W9-AAS-050

Smile

Raina Telgemeier

with color by Stephanie Yue

graphix

An Imprint of

■SCHOLASTIC

New York Toronto London Auckland Sydney Mexico City New Delhi Hong Kong

Copyright © 2010 by Raina Telgemeier

All rights reserved. Published by Graphix, an imprint of Scholastic Inc., Publishers since 1920. SCHOLASTIC, GRAPHIX, and associated logos are trademarks and/or registered trademarks of Scholastic Inc. All other trademarks are the property of their respective owners and are used without permission.

No part of this publication may be reproduced, stored in a retrieval system, or transmitted in any form or by any means, electronic, mechanical, photocopying, recording, or otherwise, without written permission of the publisher. For information regarding permission, write to Scholastic Inc., Attention: Permissions Department, 557 Broadway, New York, NY 10012.

This graphic novel is based on personal experiences, though some names have been changed, and certain characters, places, and incidents have been modified in service of the story.

Library of Congress Cataloging-in-Publication Data
Telgemeier, Raina.
Smile / Raina Telgemeier. – 1st ed.
p. cm.
ISBN: 978-1-338-17963-7
1. Youth–Dental care. 2. Girls–Dental care. 3. Self-esteem in adolescence.
4. Beauty, Personal. 5. Graphic novels. I. Title.
RK55.Y68.T45 2010
617.6'45–dc22
2008051782
10 9 8 7 6 5 4 3 2 1   16 17 18 19 20

First edition, February 2010
Edited by Cassandra Pelham
Book design by Phil Falco and John Green
Creative Director: David Saylor
Printed in Malaysia 108

For Dave

3

27

CHAPTER TWO

33

They had to give me several novocaine shots because they kept wearing off and things would start to hurt.

THERE WE GO.

Once the roots in your teeth have been cleaned out, they fill the holes that were drilled in each tooth with cement.

YOU'RE ALMOST DONE!

THTK'S GFDK...

The cement is sealed with a red-hot metal tool...

...which I SMELLED as it accidentally touched the roof of my mouth before I felt it.

HISSSSS

OOOOO! SORRY!

43

44

45

47

CHAPTER THREE

That summer was pretty normal, as summers go.

Girl Scout Camp

Grandma

Nintendo

Fog

Car trips

Orthodontist

IT'S SO STRANGE TO LOOK OUT OVER THE CITY WHEN ALL THE LIGHTS ARE OUT.

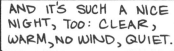
AND IT'S SUCH A NICE NIGHT, TOO: CLEAR, WARM, NO WIND, QUIET.

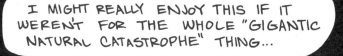
I MIGHT REALLY ENJOY THIS IF IT WEREN'T FOR THE WHOLE "GIGANTIC NATURAL CATASTROPHE" THING...

The day after that? It was BACK TO SCHOOL.

$x + 3 = 7$
$y + 6 = 11$
$x + y = ?$

Doodle Doodle

Nobody could really concentrate on class work, though... not even most of the teachers.

YOU GUYS CAN HAVE A FREE PERIOD... JUST TAKE IT EASY TODAY, OKAY?

I'M GLAD YOU'RE OKAY!

ME TOO! I MEAN, JUST IMAGINE...

WHAT IF WE'D HAD AN EARTHQUAKE WHILE SCHOOL WAS IN SESSION?!

CRUMBLE!

CHAPTER FOUR

The last day of school came and went.

HAVE A FUN CHRISTMAS!

THANKS... HAVE A NICE HANUKKAH.

Usually, the start of Winter Break is one of the most exciting times of the year.

But that year, everything served as a reminder of what was about to happen to me.

LOOK, GRANDMA GAGNON SENT US A PACKAGE!

OOH, WHAT IS IT?

...PEANUT BRITTLE!

107

108

* FROM NEW KIDS ON THE BLOCK!

118

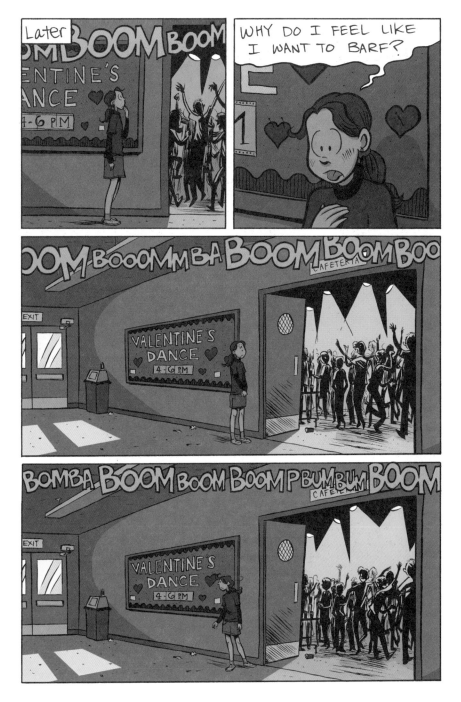

And so:
THERE! SEAN'S GOING TO LOVE IT!!
KKTHPLBBT!!!
HA HA HA
HA HA HA HA
HA Hee HA HA
HA
WAAAAIT A MINUTE...
HA HA
HA HA HA HA HA HA
HA HA HA
Hoo HA
HA Hee

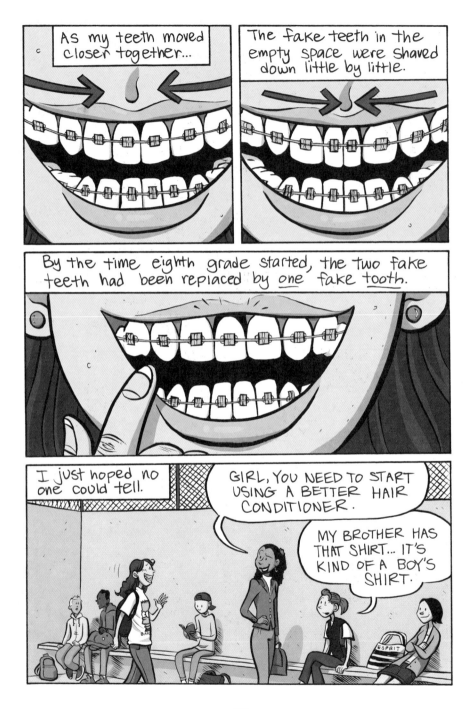

CHAPTER SIX

As my teeth moved closer together...

The fake teeth in the empty space were shaved down little by little.

By the time eighth grade started, the two fake teeth had been replaced by <u>one</u> fake <u>tooth</u>.

I just hoped no one could tell.

GIRL, YOU NEED TO START USING A BETTER HAIR CONDITIONER.

MY BROTHER HAS THAT SHIRT... IT'S KIND OF A BOY'S SHIRT.

146

My crush on Sean was old news to everyone else, but it still consumed my thoughts a lot of the time.

15... 36... SEAN...

However, something interesting was starting to happen.

HEY, RAINA!

HEY, KAYLAH. HEY, EDWARD.

YOU GOIN' TO LUNCH?

YEARBOOK ORDERS
MAR 27th

YEAH, WAIT UP.

Some of my friends had kinda-sorta-maybe boyfriends.

168

CHAPTER SEVEN

That summer, I was a Girl Scout camp counselor for the last time.

The cutest boy ♪ I ever saw was sipping ciiiiiiiider through a straw!

I also sat between my siblings in the car on a couple of long-distance road trips.

MOM!! WILL'S TOUCHING MY **FOOT**!!

178

The next stage of my orthodontic treatment was a fairly entertaining one, designed to correct my

CROSS-BITE.

(That's when your top and bottom jaws don't line up.)

To fix this, little hooks are attached to specific brackets on the top and the bottom teeth...

①
②

...and a tiny rubber band is stretched between them.

I CAN' OPEN MA MOUF ALL TH' WEY!

Twannngg!

YOU'LL GET USED TO IT!

So, tiny rubber bands joined the contents of my backpack.

Along with travel toothbrush and paste, dental wax, floss, floss-threaders, a little box of toothpicks, and a tiny bottle of mouthwash.

It was quite the spectacle when I went to get a pencil or whatever.

...OOP!

HA HA! LOOKS LIKE SOMEONE'S TRYING TO COVER UP THEIR DOG BREATH!!

CHAPTER EIGHT

But the more I focused on my interests, the more it brought out things I liked about myself.

And that affected the way other people saw me!

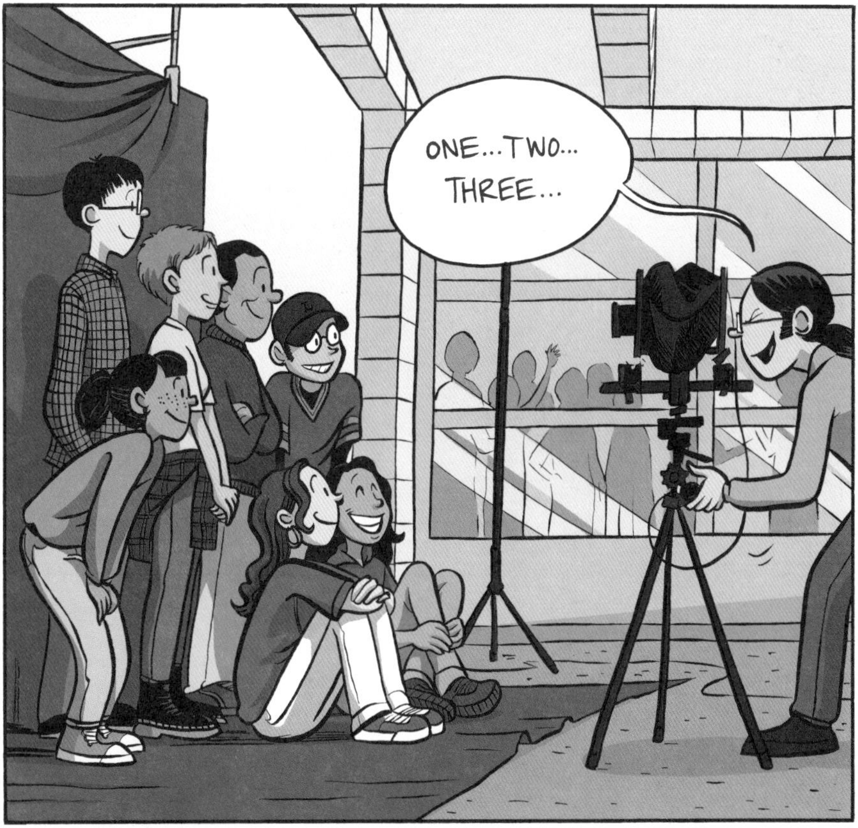
ONE... TWO...
THREE...

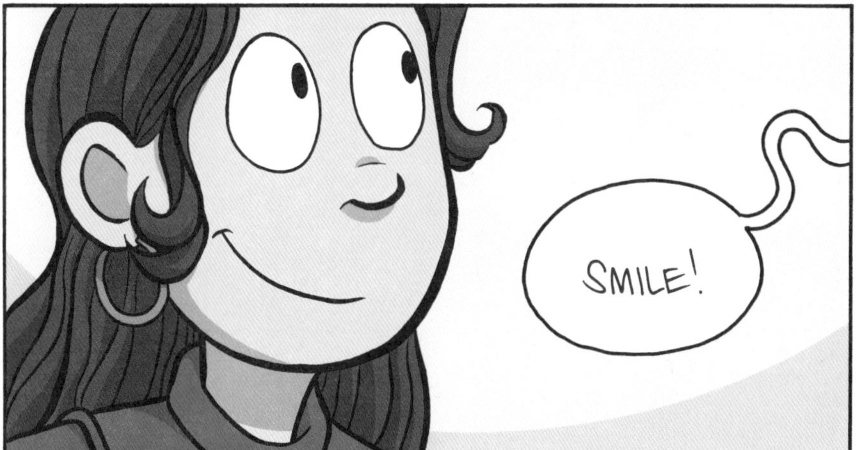
SMILE!

The End!

Thanks to...

First and foremost, Dave Roman, who makes me smile every day.

Mom, Dad, Amara, Will, and Grandma, for being good sports and a great family.

Lea Ada Franco (Hernandez), Joey Manley, and everyone at Girlamatic.com, for giving a home to this project in its infancy. My friend and family dentist, Dr. Anne Spiegel, who evaluated the manuscript and gave me great encouragement along the way. David Saylor and Cassandra Pelham, for being a joy to work with. Phil Falco, John Green, and Stephanie Yue, for helping make my work beautiful. Judy Hansen, for being the best agent I could hope to have.

Alisa Harris, Braden Lamb, Carly Monardo, Craig Arndt, Dalton Webb, Hope Larson, Jordyn Bochon, Kean Soo, Matt Loux, Naseem Hrab, Rosemary Travale, Ryan Estrada, and Yuko Ota, for lending a helping hand during the final stages of production.

All of my friends who wrote me yearbook notes.

Everyone who has shared their own personal dental dramas with me.

The city of San Francisco, for giving me great backgrounds to draw!

Archwired.com, Janna Morishima, Heidi MacDonald, and Barbara Moon, for all their support and enthusiasm over the years.

Theresa Mendoza Pacheco, Marion Vitus, Steve Flack, Alison Wilgus, Zack Giallongo, Gina Gagliano, Bannister, Steve Hamaker, Seth Kushner, Neil Babra, and my extended family, wonderful friends, and readers, who have been invaluable.

Author's Note

I've been telling people about what happened to my teeth ever since I knocked them out in sixth grade. The story had plenty of strange twists and turns, and I found myself saying, "Wait, it gets worse!" a lot. Eventually, I realized I really needed to get it all down on paper.

I had been writing short-story comics for several years, and my tooth tale seemed like a good candidate for a longer narrative comic.

In 2004 I was invited to contribute to a comics-based Web site, Girlamatic.com, and decided to run Smile as a weekly Webcomic. This was at the same time I began working on The Baby-sitters Club graphic novels for Scholastic, so the two projects grew and evolved in tandem. By the time I completed the fourth BSC graphic novel, I had drawn, serialized, and posted over 120 pages of Smile on the Web!

As I wrote and drew the story, I was able to look back and actually laugh at some of my more painful experiences. What I went through with my teeth wasn't fun, but I lived to tell the tale and came out of it a stronger person. And once Smile started to receive reader feedback, I was amazed by how many people had dental stories similar to my own! The process of creating Smile has been therapeutic for me, and has also put me in touch with hundreds of kindred spirits. For this I am very grateful.

Even though my smile looks normal now, it's very possible I'll face more dental drama in the future. Amazingly, I'm not afraid of dentists, or dental work. I have a lot of faith and trust in dentistry, and how it can improve people's lives. And on the bright side of things, beyond the work I've had done on my front teeth, I haven't had a cavity since I was six!

Thanks so much for reading.

— Raina

Raina Telgemeier is the #1 *New York Times* bestselling, multiple Eisner Award-winning creator of *Smile* and *Sisters*, which are both graphic memoirs based on her childhood. She is also the creator of *Drama*, which was named a Stonewall Honor Book and was selected for YALSA's Top Ten Great Graphic Novels for Teens. Raina lives in the San Francisco Bay Area. To learn more, visit her online at www.goRaina.com.